Level 2 is ideal for children who ha... ...ne reading instruction a... ...simple sentences v...

Special featur...

...ect

GW01451351

Short, simple sentences

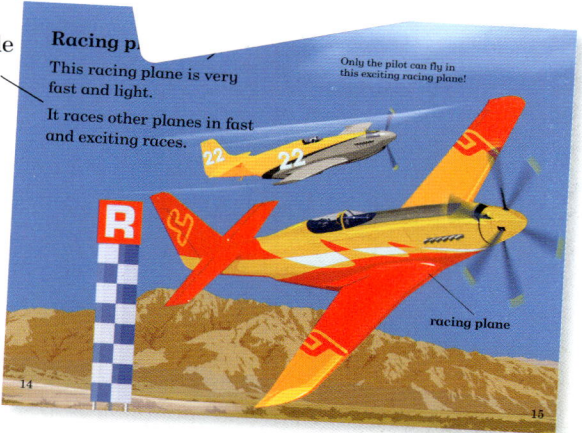

Racing p...

This racing plane is very fast and light.

It races other planes in fast and exciting races.

Only the pilot can fly in this exciting racing plane!

22

R

racing plane

14

15

Careful match between text and pictures

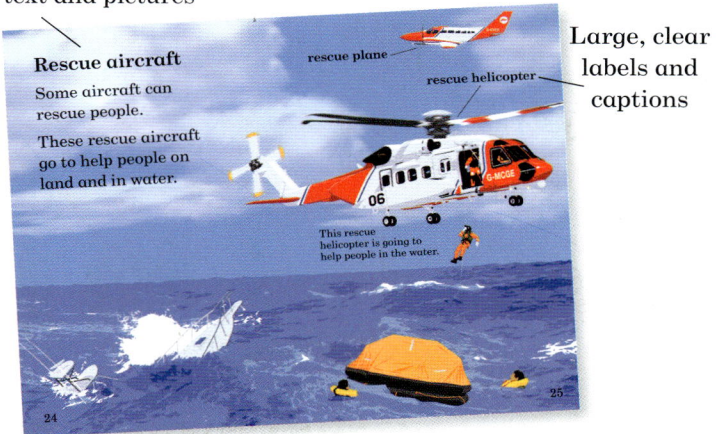

Rescue aircraft

Some aircraft can rescue people.

These rescue aircraft go to help people on land and in water.

rescue plane

rescue helicopter

Large, clear labels and captions

06

G-MCGE

This rescue helicopter is going to help people in the water.

24

25

Educational Consultant: Geraldine Taylor
Book Banding Consultant: Kate Ruttle
Subject Consultant: Ian Graham

LADYBIRD BOOKS

UK | USA | Canada | Ireland | Australia
India | New Zealand | South Africa

Ladybird Books is part of the Penguin Random House group of companies
whose addresses can be found at global.penguinrandomhouse.com.

www.penguin.co.uk www.puffin.co.uk www.ladybird.co.uk

Penguin
Random House
UK

First published 2017
001

Copyright © Ladybird Books Ltd, 2017

Printed in China

A CIP catalogue record for this book is available from the British Library

ISBN: 978-0-241-27550-4

All correspondence to
Ladybird Books
Penguin Random House Children's Books
80 Strand, London WC2R ORL

Amazing
Aircraft

Written by Catherine Baker
Illustrated by Martin Sanders

Contents

Off in a jet plane

Have you seen a plane like this one?

Many people go on holiday on a passenger jet like this.

passenger jet

These people
are going off on
holiday in a big
passenger jet.

Big planes

Some planes are very big.

This big passenger jet is called the Airbus A380.

It can fly fast and high.

Over 500 passengers can get into the Airbus A380!

Electric planes

This little Airbus plane has electric engines.

Only two people can get into this little electric plane.

pilot   passenger

This little electric plane is very light.

Airbus electric plane

13

Racing planes

This racing plane is very fast and light.

It races other planes in fast and exciting races.

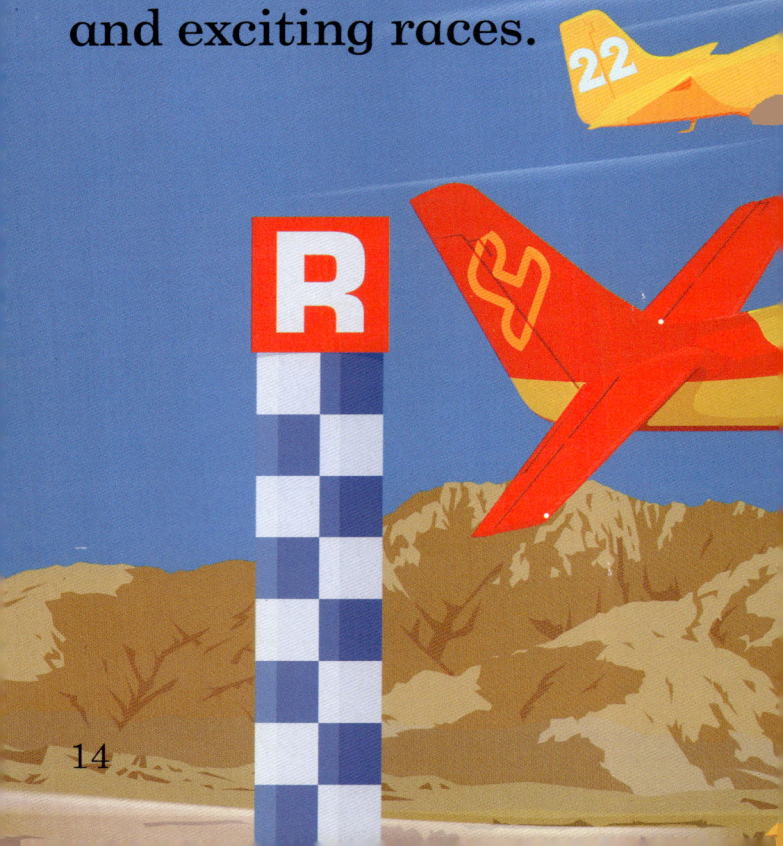

Only the pilot can fly in
this exciting racing plane!

racing plane

Fire! Fire!

This special plane is going to put out a big fire.

It races to the fire and it has water to put the fire out.

fire

water

Helicopters

You can fly in many other aircraft.

You can go high up in a helicopter, too.

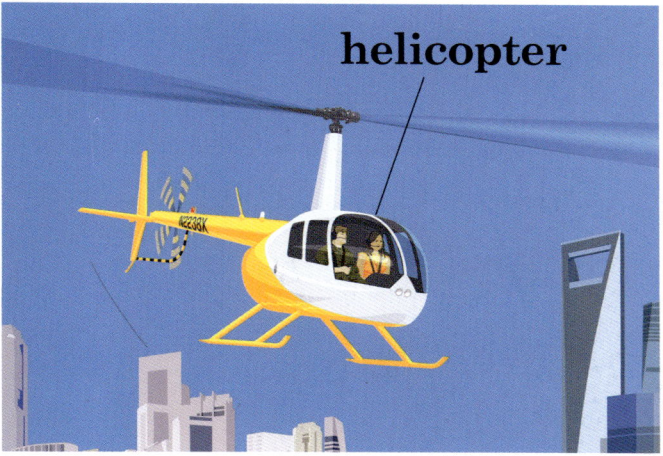

helicopter

Helicopters like these are exciting to fly in!

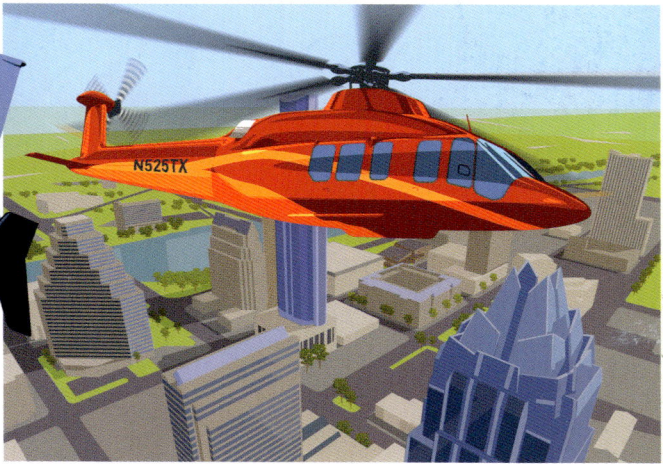

Gliders

Gliders look like planes, but they do not have engines.

glider

Would you like to go up in a glider like this one?

A plane pulls the glider up, like this.

Big airships

This very big aircraft is called an airship.

It has a light gas in it that makes the airship fly.

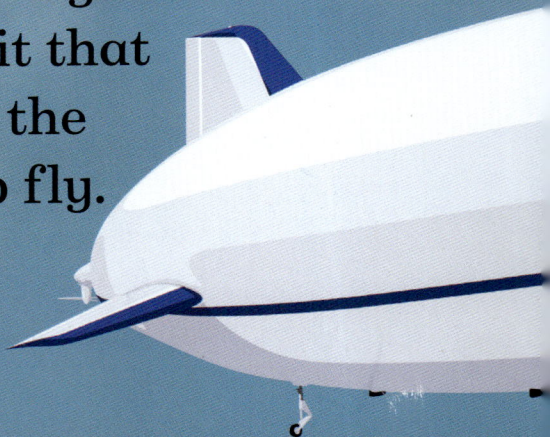

The airship has special engines
to help it take off and land.

gas is in here

engine

Rescue aircraft

Some aircraft can rescue people.

These rescue aircraft go to help people on land and in water.

rescue plane

rescue helicopter

G-EXEX

G-MCGE

06

This rescue helicopter is going to help people in the water.

25

Be a pilot!

It is exciting to be a pilot, and to fly fast planes and helicopters.

If you fly in a rescue aircraft, you can help other people, too!

pilot

The helicopter pulls up
the rescued people.

Picture glossary

Airbus A380

airship

electric plane

glider

helicopter

passenger jet

passengers

pilot

police helicopter

rescue helicopter

rescue plane

Index